Marvelous Math

A BOOK OF POEMS

Selected by **Lee Bennett Hopkins**

Illustrated by **Karen Barbour**

SCHOLASTIC INC.

New York   Toronto   London   Auckland   Sydney
Mexico City   New Delhi   Hong Kong

To Joan C. Stevenson—
because 1+1=2
—LBH

For John Marsh Davis
—KB

A note from the artist:
The illustrations were painted with Winsor & Newton gouache paint—an opaque
watercolor—on 140 lb. Arches cold-pressed watercolor paper. I usually painted
the backgrounds first, then painted the outlines for the figures in black acrylic and
colored them in, sometimes adding several layers of paint. Other times,
I used pencil for the outline and then would go over and over it
with gouache to color it in before adding more black outline.

ISBN 0-590-63240-X

12 11 10 9 8 7 6 5   9/9 0 1 2 3 4/0

Printed in the U.S.A.   14

First Scholastic printing, January 1999

The text for this book is set in 14-point Weidemann Bold.

Marvelous
Math

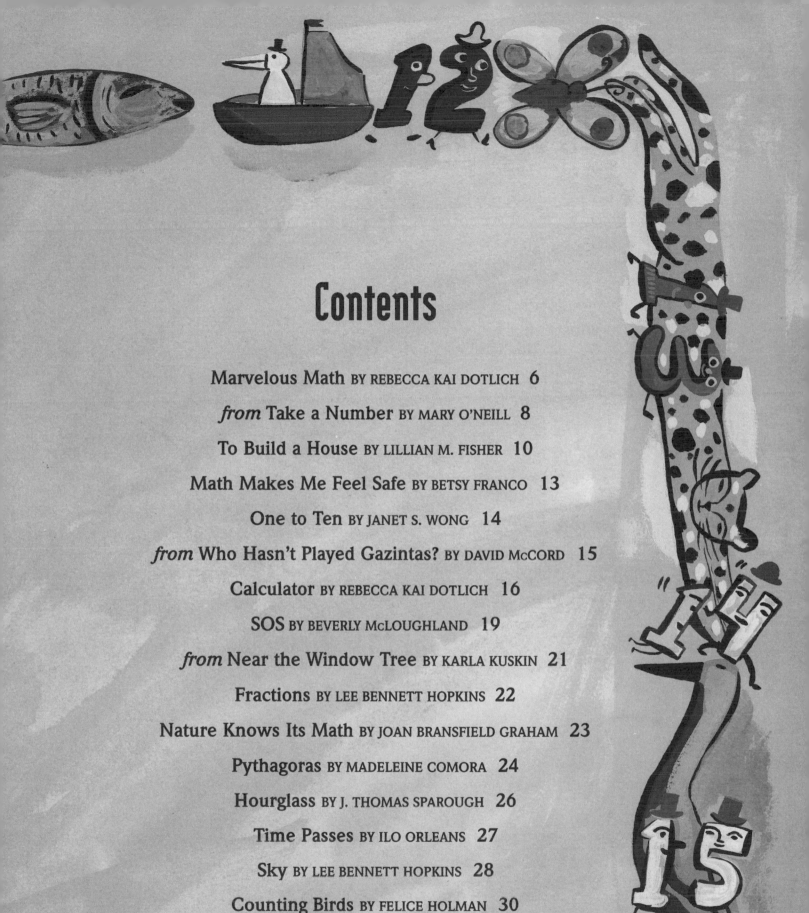

Contents

Marvelous Math BY REBECCA KAI DOTLICH 6

from Take a Number BY MARY O'NEILL 8

To Build a House BY LILLIAN M. FISHER 10

Math Makes Me Feel Safe BY BETSY FRANCO 13

One to Ten BY JANET S. WONG 14

from Who Hasn't Played Gazintas? BY DAVID McCORD 15

Calculator BY REBECCA KAI DOTLICH 16

SOS BY BEVERLY McLOUGHLAND 19

from Near the Window Tree BY KARLA KUSKIN 21

Fractions BY LEE BENNETT HOPKINS 22

Nature Knows Its Math BY JOAN BRANSFIELD GRAHAM 23

Pythagoras BY MADELEINE COMORA 24

Hourglass BY J. THOMAS SPAROUGH 26

Time Passes BY ILO ORLEANS 27

Sky BY LEE BENNETT HOPKINS 28

Counting Birds BY FELICE HOLMAN 30

MARVELOUS MATH

Rebecca Kai Dotlich

How fast does a New York taxi go?
What size is grandpa's attic?
How old is the oldest dinosaur?
The answer's in *Mathematics!*

How many seconds in an hour?
How many in a day?
What size are the planets in the sky?
How far to the Milky Way?

How fast does lightning travel?
How slow do feathers fall?
How many miles to Istanbul?
Mathematics knows it all!

from
TAKE A NUMBER

Mary O'Neill

Imagine a world
Without mathematics:

No rulers or scales,
No inches or feet,
No dates or numbers
On house or street,
No prices or weights,
No determining heights,
No hours running through
Days and nights.
No zero, no birthdays,
No way to subtract
All of the guesswork
Surrounding the fact.
No sizes for shoes,
Or suit or hat. . . .
Wouldn't it be awful
To live like that?

TO BUILD A HOUSE

Lillian M. Fisher

Here on this plot
Our house will rise
Against the hill
Beneath blue skies

Ruler and tape
Measure the size
Of windows and cupboards
The floors inside

We add, subtract,
Multiply, divide
To build closets and stairs
The porch outside

Without numbers and measure
Would our house ever rise
Against the hill
Beneath blue skies?

MATH MAKES ME FEEL SAFE

Betsy Franco

Math isn't just adding
and subtracting.
Not for me.

Math makes me feel safe
knowing that my brother will always be
three years younger than I am,
and every day of the year will have
twenty-four hours.
That a snowflake landing on my mitten
will have exactly six points,
and that I can make new shapes
from my Tangram pieces
whenever I feel lonely.

Math isn't just adding
and subtracting,
Not for me.

Math makes me feel safe.

ONE TO TEN

Janet S. Wong

Yut yee sam see
Count in Cantonese with me!

Eun look chut bot
Can you tell me what we've got?

Gow sup. One to ten!
(Could you say that once again?)

from
WHO HASN'T PLAYED GAZINTAS?

David McCord

In your arithmetics
the *problem* is what sticks.
The language isn't bound
by spelling, but by sound.
So 3 gazinta 81.
The answer? 27. Done!
In *long* division, I would hint, a
lot of work gazin gazinta.

Then Tums: the sign of which is x.
Do 8 tums 1-5-6? It checks
at just one thousand two four eight.
Repeat: 1,248.

Computers work at a faster rate.

CALCULATOR

Rebecca Kai Dotlich

Pocket-size tutor.
Mathematician.
Genius with fractions.

Mini-magician.

16

SOS

Beverly McLoughland

Sammy's head is pounding—
Sammy's in pain—
A long division's got
Stuck in his brain—
Call for the locksmith
Call the engineer
Call for the plumber
To suck out his ear,
Call the brain surgeon
To pry out the mess,
Call out the Coast Guard
SOS,
Because—
Sammy's head is pounding—
Sammy's in pain—
A long division's got
Stuck in his brain.

from
NEAR THE WINDOW TREE
Karla Kuskin

Is six times one a lot of fun?
Or eight times two?
Perhaps for you.
But five times three
Unhinges me,
While six and seven and eight times eight
Put me in an awful state
And four and six and nine times nine
Make me want to cry and whine
So when I get to twelve times ten
I begin to wonder when
I can take a vacation from multiplication
And go out
And start playing again.

FRACTIONS

Lee Bennett Hopkins

Broken number pieces
disconnected—

a quarter
a half
an eighth

fragmented—

out of order
out of control—

until—

I explore them
restore them

make them
whole
once more
again.

NATURE KNOWS ITS MATH

Joan Bransfield Graham

Divide
the year
into seasons,
four,
subtract
the snow then
add
some more
green,
a bud,
a breeze,
a whispering
behind
the trees,
and here
beneath the
rain-scrubbed
sky
orange poppies
multiply.

PYTHAGORAS
Madeleine Comora

Watching four birds fly by,
two . . .
        four . . .
              six . . .
eight wings in harmony
rising
      then
            falling,
Pythagoras said:
All things are numbers.
The universe
counted and measured
even or odd,
forms rhythmic patterns
of motion and harmony
like the beating
          wings
             of birds.

HOURGLASS

J. Thomas Sparough

Lonely waves
without a clock
once pounded
molten rock

Forever rhythm
where I stand
now estimated
in grains of sand.

TIME PASSES

Ilo Orleans

Sixty seconds
Pass in a minute.
Sixty minutes
Pass in an hour.
Twenty-four hours
Pass in a day—
And that's how TIME
Keeps passing away!

SKY
Lee Bennett Hopkins

Decimal point
meteors
streak
through
the night—

Fractions
of moonbeams
gleam
white-bright—

Percentages
of stars
seem
to multiply—

in the
finite
dramatic
mathematic-filled
sky.

COUNTING BIRDS

Felice Holman

Instead of counting herds of sheep,
Sometimes when I am going to sleep
I think of the names of birds I love—
Merlin, mud hen, mourning dove,
Willet, whimbrel, wamp, and widgeon,
Petrel, puffin, pipit, pigeon,
Hawk and auk and
Quawk and quail,
Redpoll, ricebird, reeve, ruff, rail,
Kite and kestrel, kittiwake,
Curlew, creeper, crane, and crake.

Counting the names of birds I love—
Merlin, mud hen, m
                    o
                      u
                        r
                          n
                            i
                              n
                                g
                                  d
                                    o
                                      v
                                        e. . . .

Acknowledgments

Thanks are due to the following for works reprinted herein:

Madeleine Comora for "Pythagoras."
Used by permission of the author, who controls all rights.
Curtis Brown, Ltd. for "Fractions" and "Sky" by Lee Bennett Hopkins.
Copyright © 1997 by Lee Bennett Hopkins.
Used by permission of Curtis Brown, Ltd.
Rebecca Kai Dotlich for "Calculator" and "Marvelous Math."
Used by permission of the author, who controls all rights.
Lillian M. Fisher for "To Build a House."
Used by permission of the author, who controls all rights.
Betsy Franco for "Math Makes Me Feel Safe."
Used by permission of the author, who controls all rights.
Joan Bransfield Graham for "Nature Knows Its Math."
Used by permission of the author, who controls all rights.
Felice Holman for "Counting Birds" from *At the Top of My Voice
and Other Poems.* Copyright © 1971 by Charles Scribner's Sons.
Little, Brown and Company for an excerpt from "Who Hasn't Played
Gazintas?" from *One at a Time* by David McCord. Copyright © 1952 by
David McCord. Used by permission of Little, Brown and Company.
Margaret K. McElderry Books for "One to Ten" from *Good Luck Gold
and Other Poems* by Janet S. Wong. Copyright © 1994 by Janet S. Wong.
Reprinted with the permission of Margaret K. McElderry Books,
an imprint of Simon & Schuster Children's Publishing Division.
Beverly McLoughland for "SOS."
Used by permission of the author, who controls all rights.
Marian Reiner for an excerpt from *Take a Number* by Mary O'Neill.
Copyright © 1968 by Mary O'Neill. Copyright renewed 1996 by
Erin Baroni and Abagail Hagler. Reprinted by permission of Marian Reiner.
Karen Solomon for "Time Passes" by Ilo Orleans.
J. Thomas Sparough for "Hourglass."
Used by permission of the author, who controls all rights.
Scott Treimel New York for "Is Six Times One a Lot of Fun"
from *Near the Window Tree* by Karla Kuskin.
Copyright © 1975 by Karla Kuskin.
Reprinted by permission of Scott Treimel New York.

The answer to the long division problem on page 18 is 241486140.6